MW00674692

This Book Belongs To:

A WOMAN in MINISTRY

DEDICATION

This book is dedicated to all my sisters in
ministry and to the women who encouraged
me to soar and released me to do ministry
Dorothy C. Johnson, my mother
Sister Adelaide L. Sanford, my village mother
Susan L. Taylor, my Sag Harbor/Isis sister
Bertha Williams, my adopted aunt
Melody, Mercedes and Sidney,
my prayer partners

And, it is dedicated to Dr. Ollie B. Wells,
Dr. A.C.D. Vaughn, Bishop John Bryant,
Dr. Wyatt Tee Walker, and "Dad" Mason
who helped me exercise my gifts.

The SISTER'S RULES *for* Ministry

Rev. Dr. Suzan D. Johnson Cook

ALSO BY SUZAN JOHNSON COOK

Wise Women Bearing Gifts: *Joys and Struggles of Their Faith*, editor

Preaching in Two Voices: *Sermons on the Women in Jesus' Life* (with William D. Watley)

Sister to Sister Devotions: *Devotions for and from African American Women*, editor

Sister Strength: *A Collection of Devotionals for and from African-American Women*, editor

Too Blessed to Be Stressed: *Words of Wisdom for Women on the Move*

A New Dating Attitude: *Getting Ready for the Mate God Has for You*

Praying for the Men in Your Life

The SISTER'S RULES for Ministry

The Sister's Rules for Ministry
Copyright © 2003 by Rev. Dr. Suzan D. Johnson Cook
and Adrienne Ingrum

Other translation quoted:
The King James Version (KJV).

Printed in Canada

Cover design by Byfieldesign

Library of Congress Control Number: 2003102280
ISBN: 1-889732-46-X

This book was proudly produced by

Word For Word Publishing Co., Inc.
Brooklyn, NY 11201
718-222-WORD (9673)
1-800-601-WORD

Visit our website at: www.WordForWord.us

E-mail us at: info@WordForWord.us

For order information, see last page.

CONTENTS

INTRODUCTION

On Wednesday, June 5, 2002 I was honored to be elected by my 8,000 peers and colleagues as the first female president of the historic Hampton University Ministers' Conference, the largest gathering of African-American clergy in the world. It was a wonderfully blessed and anointed moment, and I felt as though God had prepared me, as the book of Esther says, "for such a time as this." (Esther 4:14) In the chapel, where the voting occurred, were hundreds of my sisters who had prayed and hoped for this moment, as well as thousands of my brothers who had made this their mission. One retired pastor now in his eighties, Rev. Charles Green of Arlington, Virginia, kissed me and said, "I asked the Lord to allow me to see this moment."

"Wow! God has done this!" I marveled.

Life and ministry as I had known it would never be the same. The next sixty days were filled with telegrams, phone calls, letters, flowers, and other congratulatory expressions from around the country. Leaders of conventions, which had historically been closed to women, called me for interviews for their magazines, as well as to extend invitations to me to make remarks at their annual meetings and conventions. They all addressed me as "Madame President" and pledged their private and public support.

A few weeks subsequent to all of this, Pastor Marvin McMickle published an encyclopedia of African-American religious leaders (*An Encyclopedia of African-American Christian Heritage*, Judson Press). As I flipped it open, there was my picture opposite Dr. James Forbes, one of my professors during divinity school training.

It humbled me to read my life story encapsulated in the text. God had clearly been preparing me to be a trailblazer. I felt the tremendous responsibility that comes with being a leader of leaders. Now that God has enlarged my tent (Isaiah 54:2), I realize I am charged to share the tremendous blessings I've been exposed to through the decades. That charge leads me to write this book for other women who are currently in or are being called by God to Christian leadership.

At age twenty-three, I gave my life and ministry to the Lord and have never looked back. After twenty-two years of ministry–twenty of those in pastoral leadership–I'm now as comfortable in a grassroots setting eating crabs on newspaper as I am at an eight-course dinner with ambassadors in Wales, England, and everything in between. Yet, I'd still rather have Jesus than anything this world offers. It's been an awesome journey, filled with excitement, adventure, warfare, struggle, victory, losses and gains. I truly have been "on the battlefield for my Lord." But the storm is passing over, Hallelujah!

I come from a family of leaders and entre-preneurs–male and female. The womb of a strong Christian woman leader, Dorothy C. Johnson, birthed me. Mom was a trailblazer in community education and entrepreneurship. She comes from a strong female leader, Leona F. Starnes Thomas, whom we called "Mama." And they descended from powerful women, many of whom learned their "sister's rules" in the fields. It's my joy to be part of a generation of women who can now get up off our knees and stand.

These are some of the rules I've learned that will help women in ministry and Christian leadership survive and thrive. I share them so that "your ways shall be prosperous and you shall have good success." (Joshua 1:8)

One last word before I share the "sister's rules for ministry." Many think a woman has to be strong all by herself, but I've had terrific men in my life all the way, from my father Wilbert T. Johnson, to my husband Ronald Cook, and even to my sons Samuel David and Christopher Daniel, and to such colleagues and mentors as Bishop T. D. Jakes, Dr. Walter Scott Thomas, Dr. Ollie B. Wells, Dr. James Forbes, Dr. Gardner C. Taylor, Dr. Dennis Proctor and a host of others who are my brother-friends. These men taught me many of the unwritten rules any woman must learn to thrive in a man's world. Before you learn the sister's rules of ministry, celebrate the men in your life! Take note of what they have already taught you.

The "sister's rules for ministry" are ten rules every woman in ministry needs to survive or the ten steps any Christian woman in leadership needs to thrive.

Rule One

It's All About God

Matthew 6:33

"...but seek ye first the Kingdom of God and His righteousness, and all these things shall be added unto you..."

With each new position of leadership, it is easier and easier to think that the world centers around us, when the foremost reality in ministry remains that the world centers around God. I must constantly remind myself that I am a spiritual being, who is trying to tap into God so that my mind will be transformed and not conformed to the me-first, it's-all-about-me attitude of this world. (See Romans 12)

A lot of Christian sisters have the attitude that ministry owes us. No one owes us a thing–especially not God. It is up to us to walk into our season. Seasons are times of opportunity given to us by God, according to *God's* timing. They don't last very long, but when God has created a season for us, we need to do something fruitful–seize, even squeeze, but make sure we give glory to God.

I applaud sisters who have answered the call to ministry or Christian leadership. I celebrate, I encourage, I will work with you, I'm prepared to mentor, but you've got to learn the rules. When

I started playing basketball, as a teenager, so much of the game I learned from males. I had to watch a few times before I got on the court. I had to read the rules, I had to go to practices, and sometimes sit on the sidelines. I didn't just start playing the game. Sisters, when you got the call, if you said, "I'm going to go out there and the world is going to be changed by what I have to say," you have to learn it's not all about you. You need what I call a "mind makeover." We know about these for makeup and hair, but as women in ministry, we often need spiritual makeovers, where our minds, the insides of us–rather than our outward appearance–are changed.

Yes, we've faced opposition to our calling. Yes, we've encountered challenges to our leadership. Yes, we've struggled to acquire training. Yes, obstacles have hindered us from fully using our gifts. But our ministry is still not about what we want, what we deserve or even what is "rightfully ours" in comparison to our male colleagues. It is all about God. We must learn the rules and be "coached" by God. We, too, may have to sit on the sidelines for a while. That may mean an unpaid assistant position. However, that's a great place to learn the rules.

God Is First

Many told me not to leave the 1,000-member historic congregation in downtown Manhattan and go to a start-up, store-front church in the Bronx. "You're making great money, you're highly visible, why leave?" But God had called me, God said, "Go." It was a new assignment. This was not their call. It was God's. The Psalmist's words reminded me that it wasn't about me; it was about God. "We are His people and the sheep of His pasture." (Psalm 100:3) This verse suggested that *I* didn't even belong to me! Against all the nay-sayers, I went. In six months the Sunday morning attendance and finances had tripled.

All that we have or even hope to be, belongs to God. Whoever we are is not accidental, nor are the experiences we've had coincidences. God has orchestrated every move, even those things we define as conflict. The ministries in which we find ourselves are God's placements. "I know the plans I have for you," declares the LORD, "plans to prosper you and not to harm you, plans to give you hope and a future." (Jeremiah 29:11)

Because we live in a mega-church, mega-media-ministry age, many of us think we've failed when we're not operating at that level. But God needs people in *all* places. Isaiah 54:3 says, "...inhabit the desolate cities." Otherwise, who would be there for those who are "off the beaten path"? The church I pastor currently is not on a main street, but people have found it. God has led them there. Look for God everywhere. Listen for God in everything. Silence does not mean the absence of God. It often precedes a mighty move of God. Before the shouts and the fall of the walls of Jericho, there was, first, marching in silence. (Joshua 6:10) Let God in and let God win. He called us not so that we would be successful, but that He would be successful.

But, Don't Neglect Your Family

God first does not mean your family second. God is *not* the congregation, the sermon, the trustees meeting, the mission trip. Be intentional about making your family your first *people* priority. Plan and spend quality time with them. Ministry is demanding, but you are a woman before you are a woman minister, and before your responsibilities as a minister, you have a God-given responsibility to your family as wife, daughter, sister or mother. Worshiper, wife, mother, minister is the godly ranking of priorities if you are married with children.

It's very hard for mothers to understand that our husbands come before our children. "Those kids are my blood..." a mother once said, "...my connection to my husband is not as deep as that." This commonly-held view is simply not scriptural. No matter how deep our tie to our children, the husband-wife connection is the relationship that most mirrors God's relationship to us. It is very easy for busy, successful women to place a higher priority on those who obviously need us–our children–than on that grown man who is perfectly capable of taking care of himself. Check yourself, sisters. God first, then your man. Don't put your husband off sexually or neglect his emotional needs. Plan regular dates–things he likes to do and things you enjoy doing together. Ask your husband to stand with you, and thank him for the times he's been there for and with you. If you've blown it in the past, today is the first day of the rest of your life. Stop right now and appreciate a family man. Show him that you love him.

Leave your work at work. Have a clear separation of office and home. Don't always drag your children to midweek evening services and to business meetings or insist your husband appear at every service or gathering. When appreciation is shown to you, for example on pastoral appreciation day, or his birthday, make sure love is spread his way. (Proverbs 31:23, "Her husband is respected at the city gate...")

Take exciting vacations–without church members and nannies. I cannot tell you the expression of joy on my kids' faces when we told them we were going on a cruise last Spring break, and they learned that it was just going to be "Mom, Dad and *us*!" They had lots of uninterrupted time with their Mom and got to see their parents interact affectionately without being "on."

Family space is sacred space. Boundaries are needed for your family. Protect them from the painful moments where, for example, you vent your feelings about the church meeting and about who opposed you. You'll get over it. Families take it personally and never forget, or it takes a long time. Life is painful enough. Protect them when you can.

Take several moments to unwind before you enter your home. Some days I just sit in the garage for a few extra minutes to clear my head. In the early morning I get up before the family, and do my three-mile "meditational walk" to clear my head. So, when we interact, most of the time, I'm able to talk with them and not *at* them.

Your family is not the pastor's aide society. You are a unique unit, placed together by God. "God first, spiritually. Family first, socially.

These rules are harder than the Ten Commandments! Sister-Pastor, what about *me*?" you're probably asking.

Read on. The next rules are all about you.

Rule Two

Stay Responsible for Your Own Spiritual Groove

3 John 2

"I wish above all things that your soul prosper."

Women in ministry are on the front lines. We work hard, give to everyone else and then burn out, feel depleted, and are not replenished. Life balance is an area many women in ministry do not handle well. We preach about it to others, but many of us fail to live it and find ourselves fragmented and falling apart. Scripture says God is able to keep us from falling (Jude), yet, many of us have fallen. As I reflect on my 22 years in ministry, I am saddened that many of the women who started with me, and particularly those in the pastoral ministry, have fallen by the wayside. They've not just stopped pastoring; they've totally dropped out of God's service. They are M.I.A. (missing in action), "off the scene." Often it was because these women had no support system.

When we have few supports, we have to learn how to create them. Women in ministry are not often mentored by men. We are rarely mentored by women because there haven't been many women ministers ahead of us, and the few are so busy holding themselves together that they don't have energy to mentor all the women answering the call of God today and asking for our help.

I get a huge number of letters asking me to mentor. I ask myself, "How many people can you mentor effectively?" I have begun quarterly workshops, which I call "sister shops," forums for women in ministry. I bring together the best and the brightest ministers I have been exposed to–from conservative to liberal and everything in between–to share their stories of the success and failure. (You do fail on your way to success. It's all part of the journey.)

Being responsible for your own spiritual groove is taking the time you need for wholeness. One way that I keep my spiritual groove is just by looking at and living near the water. Our family recently moved to a lovely apartment by the water. We looked at lots of houses and apartments and decided that what we needed was light and water. This bright, airy place lets us wake up every day and see the water. I cannot tell you how soothing that is. It's hard to start a bad day.

I also recently took a four-day trip to the Caribbean to splash, sun, and be regenerated. Know what works for you, and be intentional in getting it.

Everyone is different. Discover what makes you happy, what brings you joy and brings you peace and calm. Know yourself and take the time you need to keep yourself in balance.

Balance is also about simple things. For me, it is taking time to just eat lunch without doing business, leaving my office, my desk. When it's nice out, I go for a walk so I can get some sunshine and air, but, regardless of the weather, I intentionally take time away from the office. That helps me keep my spiritual groove or get it back if it's out of whack.

If somebody has made me angry or really pushed that last button, or if I've been counseling someone and some of their energy has transferred to me, I take time to debrief. I've learned to cut my counseling load in half, no matter how dire the needs of others seem. I also count to ten or twenty after a very heated session with someone. Sounds simplistic, but it works.

A biblical woman who took responsibility for her spiritual groove was Deborah in Judges 4. I like her because she understood time management well. She stood under the palm tree and did not run back and forth to judge the people. Rather, the people from Ramah and the people from Bethel came to her for judgment. As women in ministry, we already have a lot on our plates and we must know how to manage our time well. Your ministry to yourself is determined by how you manage your time. This is very important because if you are a vessel being used by God, you have to be in a useful condition.

The other thing I like about Deborah is that she chose her battles wisely. Part of keeping your spiritual groove is understanding that you don't need to be in everybody's battle, everybody's business. Nor does everyone need to be in yours.

Deborah was clear that this was the one that God had prepared her for so this was the moment that she moved. Attend only to the concerns you hear God clearly assign to you. Be sure you know God's voice. Spend time with God and move by assignment.

Get Fit to Handle the Load

Many times we lose our spiritual groove because we are not fit to handle the load God has given us to carry. Sisters in ministry, many of us look old and out of shape, and tire out easily. I'm tall and I can carry my weight, as they say, but in almost 22 years, I had gone up to a size 22 dress, from a size 12 when I started pastoring. I was disgusted with myself and I made a decision that I was not going to buy another size 22 dress.

I looked at my congregants and reflected on those of my previous parish. In both, there were women in their 20s and 30s who looked much older because of extra weight. I prayed and asked God to show me what to do, and then initiated a "fine, fit and fabulous" ministry of health information, education and motivation. In a year our congregation collectively lost over 800 pounds. Every Sunday I provided a time for people to stand up and tell what they did to create a healthier lifestyle. They drank more water, ate only fistfuls of food, jogged, exercised, and took the stairs instead of the elevator. From sharing stories, others got ideas.

I participated in this initiative, of course. In the last year I've lost 20 pounds, come down about two dress sizes, and lost several inches. I've cut out some red meat and cut down the amount of starchy foods that I eat. I sometimes get up at 5 a.m. and walk three miles on the track. An added benefit is that I have developed new friendships among those who walk there in the morning. Because I have very small ankles, long legs and a big frame, my ankles tend to hurt and twist when I get too heavy and try to exercise. But I was determined. I hired a personal trainer. It is extremely expensive, but I am seeing the results and feeling wonderful. It's taken a long year and a half to drop 20 pounds. My goal is to drop 40. I will then be at my wedding weight, my pre-baby weight, and will be able to get back into my 14s and 16s, which is my goal. I've got a ways to go but I'm about half way there.

Fine, Fit, and Fabulous

People now stop me and say, "Wow, you're really losing weight!" That's an incentive, for although this has been a health move, it has also been a self-esteem move. Many women in ministry have been beaten down and have self-esteem issues. Sexism is real; it's systemic. Sexism is built into the history and fabric of the church and many well-meaning Christians don't even understand that they are being sexist. Women have been left out of Christian leadership so long that those of us in such roles today have, often without realizing it, absorbed some of the sexist thinking and defined ourselves by it. To be beautiful *and* a leader seemed mutually exclusive.

I believe Jesus died for us to have life and have it more abundantly. (John 10:10) That means fully exercising our spiritual gifts and fully enjoying our feminine beauty. God created us beautiful in face and form. Begin to make moves that allow you to live life more abundantly, as Jesus intends. Take the risks that are necessary. Part of taking a fine, fit and fabulous stand is to make the moves that are necessary for your life, like taking the time to exercise and eat sensibly or allocating the money to join a gym or even hire a trainer. You'll feel better about yourself and, consequently, will better serve God and others.

Sometimes There Will Be Stress

Consider Dorcas in Acts 9. Dorcas was in the church, but she died before anyone discovered that she was dead. At my leadership forums for women in ministry I see women up close, and there is a lot of pain–past and present. Many are in situations where they cannot exercise their gifts, and they feel frustrated. Others are in abusive situations. Abuse is not always physical and emotional; it's also spiritual.

In January 2002, I had the most painful experience of my life. I developed hemorrhoids. I could not walk three feet without collapsing in agony. I was willing to let the doctors cut anything that they had to. That week, also, my favorite uncle died. He was the last relative on my father's side of the family. To compound the stress, my mother was in the hospital and my adult brother was away, so the entire weight of helping my aunt make funeral arrangements and discharging my mother from the hospital fell on me. Then my family asked me to do the funeral. I ended up crying through the whole funeral. Prior to this my attitude was "never let them see you sweat." My internal stress had to be stored somewhere, and it went right to my rectum. Now I recognize that sometimes people do have to see you sweat. It's not healthy to hide and deny stress. I had to learn ways to discover what was I allowing to stress me out. I made a decision at the end of that ordeal that part of maintaining my spiritual groove was that I could not, and would not, perform family funerals again. Emotionally it takes too great a toll on me.

For some, it's not the family members who die, but those who are alive that bring on stress. A good friend, Rev. Jackiel Green, wrote a book titled *Lord, Deliver Me from Family* (JGM Ministries, Redlads, California, copyright 2001), that has proved to be a good resource for many sisters in ministry.

Examine your stressors and make the decisions that will enable you to live abundantly. You're responsible for your spiritual groove. Your physical and emotional health are what help keep you grooving.

Rule Three

Play, As You Pray
Without Ceasing

1 Thessalonians 5:17

"pray without ceasing…"

No matter how much you've planned your ministry, trusted God, and worked to hold yourself and others together, life happens. "Stuff" happens. Sometimes we get more than we asked for; sometimes all hell breaks loose. Spiritual warfare is real. Some people are mean. There are wicked spirits in this world, some assassins whose mission is to attack you. Your own physical and emotional desires can stir up a spiritual battle.

In everything, and through it all, you've got to pray. Prayer puts to use the whole armor of God, (Ephesians 6) and you must go out with your armor on. Prayer is the greatest and most important spiritual discipline. Just as a human cannot live without breathing, a Christian cannot survive without praying. A Christian female leader must pray before the meeting, during the meeting, and after the meeting. She should maintain this posture even for the meetings in which she was strategically left out. But God has the final answer, and through prayers, God hears. 2 Chronicles 20:15 lets you know the Lord *will* fight for you.

Prayer also must be accompanied by praise. God inhabits the prayers and praises of His people. "The fervent prayer of a righteous (wo)man availeth much." (James 5:16)

Prayer helps us keep our focus, and we need to stay focused no matter what. I see many sisters defeated by their lack of discipline. Their energies are so divided that they never realize their full potential. Stay focused by staying prayed up. That doesn't mean close the door on everyone and everything for hours every day–unless intercessory prayer *is* your ministry calling. Instead, staying prayed up or praying without ceasing means learning to *play as well as we pray*.

Somewhere in our Christian tradition, a subliminal message has crept in, that to have fun is a sin. Many of us feel guilty about taking time for ourselves and taking time off.

One of my Christian friends in the secular world said once, in passing, "I take my birthday off every year." On my 40th birthday, I was preaching revival in Phoenix, Arizona. I loved the people and the revival was very effective. They even sang "happy birthday" at the beginning of the service. But no one significant to me was there. I felt totally on the giving end. My friend's words came back to me, and thereafter, I started taking my birthday off.

I have learned that I need to receive as well as give. We receive from God but also from being with others. My book, *Sister to Sister*, includes a meditation called "A Sisterly Celebration" written by a young woman, Joanne Stevens, who describes healing that occurs when women get together just to have fun. Make prayer part of your fun and social affairs.

A group called Isis Women is a gathering of Black women who are on the front lines of various professions. Every other month, we have breakfast together for two hours and make sure that we don't become unglued as we are trying to help others. We start and end the day with prayer. Each sister shares one celebration in her life, or answered prayer and one prayer request.

Another way I pray and play is cruising. My husband and I love the water, and we take cruises every year. This past year we put together a cruise–the Too Blessed to Be Stressed Cruise–and urged others, particularly women in ministry, to take some time off.

To hold yourself together, you must go apart–away from your regular routine. I now understand why Jesus was at the wedding–to have fun. And He often went off on His own, away from the crowds and even His disciples, to enjoy His own and His Father's companionship. Sometimes we need to be refueled or our engines will burn out.

Rule Four

Stay Put

Psalm 46:10

"Be still and know that I am God."

When the psalmist declares these words, he's relating a message like this from God, "Stay put so that I might speak to you. You've been so busy, I haven't had a chance to tell you what I need to tell you or make contact with you." Even before the great miracle of the Red Sea, God commanded Moses and the people to stand *still* and see the salvation of the Lord.

If we're not still enough, God will wake us up from our sleep or maybe we'll find ourselves on our backs, ill. We, who are called to ministry, must be still, or as popular lingo puts it, "chill."

Stay put even if it means you're not on everybody's preaching list and agenda. I've learned that rather than ask God for more, ask God, "Have I completed my assignment that You've given me? Have I done the best I could with what You've placed in my hands?" Be in a posture for a productive move, poised and ready for a move of the Holy Spirit. By staying put, the seed–God's purpose–doesn't stop growing in you. It's God's time to germinate the seed so that you can grow, and grow in a healthy direction. Staying put also allows God to weed out what stagnates your growth.

I'm so used to the "main strip" that I almost missed a period of rest, reflection and renewal God gave me by not appreciating the remote places where I have been invited to preach. Believe me, some were out-of-the-way places I'd rather not have been, where all I could do was be still.

If there is a common tragedy I see with my sisters in ministry, it is that we move too fast and veer off course. Most of the time this stems from an ego need or competition—the desire to be like someone or to have as much as we perceive someone else has. But God designs each of us uniquely to handle what God has put on our plate.

Remember the show "Mission Impossible"? "It's your mission if you choose to accept it..." was the preamble to the description of each mission. Many women in ministry don't know the mission. We're all over the place and we disguise it in the name of the Lord. Then, we become bitter when we see others whose ministries are flourishing.

Staying put allows God to reveal to you what God desires you to do. One of my favorite activities at school was plaster of Paris. We made different designs, sometimes a hand print or a flower. The mold was not useful until the object to be imprinted stayed put long enough for the plaster to harden. God makes a print on our lives, a hand print. God said in Isaiah 49:16, "I've engraved you on the palms of my hand." But the print cannot solidify if we do not take time.

Robert Pulley, one of my favorite pastors, suggests we tithe a tenth day—just as we tithe our dollars. One of every ten days is given to the Lord for consecration. With busy life styles, few of us can take a full day but we *can* make part of that day totally God's. I've started, and I can't get a full day in, but I can usually get in one to three hours of totally listening to God, not even talking. This "stay put" time is without the phone, without talking to friends, without the television, just being still. What God has begun to reveal to me in those consecration times has been phenomenal. I've received confirmation on some things that I needed to know from God, from direction to move our congregation physically to a new location, and guidance to move them spiritually to another place.

God will reveal, when you stay put.

Rule Five

Be Arrested by the Holy Spirit

Zechariah 4: 6

"Not by might, nor by power, but by my Spirit"
says the LORD Almighty.

Bishop Neil Ellis, at the Millennium Pastors Conference in Nassau, Bahamas said, "You were brought here to be arrested by the Holy Spirit. The Holy Spirit can hold you in a place where you can't escape."

That's what I want. I want to be arrested by the Holy Spirit so that I am clear, not only on who I am and whose I am, but on the direction I am to go. Some of us have been so well-trained academically, that we attempt to act based on our intellect, but "'Not by might, or by power, but by my Spirit' says the LORD Almighty" according to Zechariah 4:6.

My prayer for you is that you will be so filled by God's Spirit that you will feel under arrest.

Rule Six

Leadership Doesn't Confer Maturity

1 Corinthians 13:11

"When I was a child I thought as a child but when I became a man, when I became a woman, I put away childish ways."

Children are busy. They're into this one minute, and that the next. However, a mature adult is focused and will finish a project before going on to the next. My sisters, it's time to mature. Mature in your spiritual life, temperament, and especially in your desires. Desire what God has for you. "Not my will but thy will be done, oh Lord." Let your experiences and life lessons mature you before you seek your next assignment from God.

Ephesians 4:14 says, "don't be like children tossed to and fro." Henri Nouwen in the Genesse Diary (Doubleday Image Books, New York, copyright 1976) speaks of how often we become so enthralled with a new project that we forget what God gave us to do initially. In order to mature, we need to focus on our God-given tasks, no matter how basic or humble, and allow God to complete in us what He has begun.

Rule Seven

Don't Sleep Your Way to a Pulpit or Be Afraid to Say "No!"

1 Chronicles 16:22

"Do not touch my anointed ones;
do my prophets no harm."

The popular NIKE company slogan says, "Just Do It." Nike's commercials and ads show that swoosh symbol and the words "Just Do It." I would take that swoosh and put the slash through it, then say to sisters in ministry, "Just *Don't* Do It!" Females in ministry are challenged to raise the standard, so that those with whom we relate understand that we are not sex objects, but rather spiritual leaders.

Because so few have had generations of women in ministry to interact with, many do not know that they are touching the anointed when they make inappropriate sexual overtures. People in the church may hurt you by making negative assumptions. Colleagues may indicate that they want you for their sexual pleasure. They may place in your hands or slip into your coat pocket the key to their rooms at conventions, for example. Firmly return it with a "No thank you." Keep your focus, stay put and maintain your spiritual groove. And just don't do it.

Some sisters need to repent. Those few thought that the way to the pulpit was the same route some women in Hollywood or in corporate America took to the board room–through the bedroom. In ministry, that is a sure way to lose your anointing–that special spiritual "extra" that the Holy Spirit sends upon God's chosen vessels to accomplish God's work. It is what adds "flavor" to those who are the salt of the earth. You also lose the respect of those with whom you will be on this journey of Christian leadership.

I entered ministry at 23, tall, slim and single. Several colleagues offered regularly to take care of my sexual needs, and, thank God, I had enough spiritual sense to decline. A handful of wonderful older men, whom I call my angels unaware, said, "Sue, you've got a reputation, an entire lifetime at stake. Don't make that move."

Women in ministry, don't lose your lifetime reputation for a two-minute man. Before you have dressed, the word will have gone out that you are easy, loose and unfit for the kingdom.

Wait for God to provide your husband or choose celibacy if that is your calling. Become Ms. Right while you're waiting for Mr. Right. You won't connect with Mr. Right by being Ms. Wrong. (*A New Dating Attitude,* Suzan Johnson Cook, Zondervan, Grand Rapids, Michigan copyright 2001) I cannot say it any more clearly than my grandmother, "Keep your legs together, your skirt down and your pants up and let God bless you."

Never allow people to confuse your role and mission. I can honestly say that in 22 years of ministry I have not had sex with my colleagues. As a result, when I stand in their pulpits to proclaim the gospel of Jesus Christ, it is unadulterated. I can face their wives and families with a clean and open heart, without any hindering emotions, because I have not been with their husband and father. We're in a traditionally male occupation, so a lot of men will telephone us and vice versa. We need to be able to have that interaction, without any eyebrows raised and with no questions.

One important development in the new paradigm of ministry in this 21st century is that many pastors are encouraging our families to know each other. Our spouses and children have gotten to know one another. Dr. Joe Ratliff from Brentwood Baptist Church in Houston did something tremendous for me. He was the first pastor to extend an invitation, including travel, to my spouse and me. (This was before we had children.) He said, "Doing ministry for me should not pull you away from your family." He was the first pastor to show me that we should fly families in together. I don't have to come back and tell the story; Ron and my children are often part of the story. I cannot tell you what that one gesture meant to me. My husband got to meet the Joe Ratliff that I always spoke about. His wife got to see the Sujay Johnson that he always talked about. The Millennium Pastor's Conference, to which I referred earlier, was also a family retreat, and my colleagues laughed when they saw me in the mommy role for the first time, trying to keep up with 6 and 9 year olds.

The only bedroom you need to be in is yours with your spouse. If you're not married, don't play house. It dishonors the God we serve.

Rule Eight

Have Your Own
Praise Party

I Samuel 30:6

"David encouraged himself in the LORD his God."

When I was in college we had a saying, "We don't need no music." If the DJ's music stopped and we still wanted to party, we would start singing, "We don't need no music" and dance to our own singing. The environment was charged with an almost electrifying energy because each of us brought our own readiness to the party.

Even when I wasn't with the crowd and my favorite song came on the radio, I would begin to move and have a party right in the dorm room by myself.

We experience wonderful times of congregational praise, but we must also enjoy times of individual praise, even if we have to muster up the energy, the enthusiasm to praise God by ourselves. Your ability to praise will get you through the roughest days, when you are, as T. D. Jakes says, "in between mountains."

Gather other praising women and invite them to your home for a praise party. In her phenomenal book *What Happens When Women Pray* (Cook Communications, Colorado Springs, Colorado, copyright 1975, 1991), Evelyn Christenson shows how God works through prayer. As women in ministry, let's show what happens when women in ministry praise God. God does inhabit our praises. (Psalm 22:3 KJV)

It is easy for us to remain busy in ministry. Often, because we *are* women, we are assigned the most rudimentary tasks in taking care of God's business. Even the most humble sister can be uninspired to tackle such assignments and feel drained and unfulfilled after completing them. Hosting a praise party–one that is totally centered on worship–with your sisters in the Lord, or "getting your praise on" all by yourself, always puts God back as the focus of your ministry. It makes the joy of the Lord, your strength. (Nehemiah 8:10)

Rule Nine

Think Outside the Box

Isaiah 54:2

*"Dig your stakes deep, enlarge the place of your tent.
Dig your stakes deep, stretch your tent curtains wide."*

The deeper you dig your stakes, the wider your tents can be enlarged. I've discovered that many of us have not ventured far out of our geographical boundaries and many have not widened our spiritual boundaries. You can only take your ministry as far as you've been exposed. Some at my leadership forums are astonished to learn that there are mega and TV ministries led by women, that there are new kinds of leaders in global ministries who are revolutionizing the world for Christ. We must ask ourselves if we are being left behind because we have such narrow thinking in our approaches to doing God's work. My generation can't even talk the language of the hip hop culture, the youth culture. It's another lingo. We can't minister through it. Thankfully, there is Jamal Bryant in Baltimore, Maryland who is 28 years old, almost half my age. He has built a congregation of more than 6,000 members in two years. He's got a spiritual maturity that allows him to use approaches to ministry that reach some whom I will never reach. This year at the Hampton Ministers' Conference we'll have a dialogue between what we call the "elder states persons"–men and women who have been in ministry for more than twenty years–and "new voices emerging," those of this new generation. It will introduce those who have never been on the Hampton stage, but who are doing marvelous works.

I urge women to think outside of whatever your boxes are, to open the dam and let the waters begin to flow as God would have them. Don't put any restrictions on what God can do through you. Living water, like a flood, takes whatever is in its path. Get in the flow. Richard Warren, pastor of Saddleback Church and author of *The Purpose Driven Church*, (Zondervan, Grand Rapids, Michigan, copyright 1995) says it this way: "Find a spiritual wave and ride it."

One of my spiritual waves is a lunch-hour ministry. I'm very clear that my target group is African-American professionals who are un-churched. Despite some waves of doubt when we first began the weekly noontime services dubbed "Wonderful Wall Street Wednesdays," I now preach to standing-room only crowds who bless us as we bless them.

Despite opposition from strict, apostolic, Holy Ghost rollers who believe there is theological curb on dancing, our church had a dinner dance. From that experience, over 35 members of one family came to the Lord. They saw in a social setting that we were able be Christian and have a wonderful time. Today, they are one of the strongest families in our church.

If you're ministering to African-American or any professionals, especially in an urban setting, you had better understand that they are going to have a social life and/or you're going to miss the chance to introduce them to the Lord. Be open to "out of the box" ministries, so you will approach today's generation with the gospel in a fresh, relevant way. We compete on Sundays with brunches, golf, tennis, bike-a-thons, marathons and sleeping in with the newspaper and hot-buttered toast. You have to reach your crowd where they are. Ask God for direction so you do not lose the Holy Ghost in doing it, but are instead strengthened by God's Spirit.

Thinking outside the box is understanding that you have to market your ministry. Some say, "That's so secular and worldly." I say, "We've got to let people know what's available in the kingdom." Jesus used the best methodology available to Him in His time. We must too.

One of my favorite Bible passages is of the daughters of Zelophehad in Numbers 26 and 27. Their dad had no sons. They were in a patriarchal society where the sons got the inheritance. However, this man had no sons, only five daughters, Mahlah, Noah, Hoglah, Milcah and Tirzah. It was the first time in the Hebrew record that women had asked, "Where is my inheritance? Why shouldn't I have my daddy's stuff?" Today, we women in ministry are the daughters of Zelophehad. It's our day to declare, "It's my turn and I'm going to think outside of the box and receive all my Father has given me."

Because there have been no paradigms and few role models for women in ministry, this is the best time to minister. Create as you go along. I'm loving having a church setting that serves as a spiritual laboratory where God lets me try new exciting things. I just played basketball with my youth ministry, and so many of them now feel a new bond with their pastor. If they work, praise God! If they don't work, God show me!

I encourage you sisters to go a new way, think a new way, do a new thing in the Lord and never be ashamed of the gospel of Jesus Christ. "Behold, I will do a new thing; now it shall spring forth..." (Isaiah 43:19)

Rule Ten

Select Your Village Mother

— You Don't Know It All —

Titus 2:3,4

*"...teach the older women...Then they can train
the younger women..."*

A room full of sisters–a whole cadre of new preachers and a few seasoned ones–at a quarterly Black Women in Leadership Forum, affectionately named Rev. Dr. Ella Mitchell "mother of the movement." She is now more than 83 years old. She was a trailblazer for Black women in ministry. The Presbyterian Church took 35 years to ordain her. We call her "Momma Mitchell" and we give her the honor she's due. Proverbs 20:29 says, "The glory of young (wo)men is their strength, gray hair is the splendor of the old." We sat at her feet and listened as she shared what it took for us to be able to be ministry leaders. She admonished us not to use the pulpit to defend our calling, to share or bare our anger or bitterness. We must honor those who paved the way for us, sisters. Many of us don't know what it took to be in leadership in previous generations. Any woman who is successful in ministry needs to be celebrated as a sister because the stained glass ceiling is a reality, and it's not getting any lower. It needs to be shattered. It's been punctured by sisters like retired Bishop Leontine Kelly, (United Methodist Church), Barbara Harris (the first female bishop of the Episcopal Church), and Katie Cannon, the first female ordained in the Presbyterian Church, and others, but it needs to be shattered. It's been cracked, a glass that looks like a spider web, but it hasn't been shattered to pieces yet. It's going to take the collective strength and celebration of sisters in ministry for other sisters in ministry to succeed.

Every sister in ministry has to choose a spiritual village mother because none of us knows it all. And the selection is not by chronological age, but by seasoning and the favor of God. Be in a posture of learning. Remain pleasant and faithful; do not become bitter. I knew several women in ministry who recently died, having spent their last years being bitter. They had something burning inside of them that they could not release because doors were not only shut, but slammed in their faces and sealed. When the women went to the tomb of Jesus, they asked, "Who shall roll the stone away?" We must raise that question regarding our opportunities to minister and remember their answer. When they got there, the stone was already removed. It takes a woman who is spiritually sensitive, who is willing to bring her spices to serve Jesus regardless, and wait her turn. A revolution will occur in her life. Her stones will be rolled away, and doors will open for her ministry.

We think the revolution needs to happen with the men. Revolution needs to happen in us. It will... if we forego jealousy and competition, and join hands with the women who have served before us. We will learn from them "the secret of being content in any and every situation..." (Philippians 4:12), as we joyfully serve our risen Savior and Lord.

Closing Prayer

Closing Prayer for My Dear Sisters

The Lord bless you and keep you.

May God continue to use you in ways you didn't even think possible.

May you let the King of Glory into your life and ministry. Who is the King of Glory? The LORD strong and mighty, the LORD mighty in battle. (Psalm 24)

May you prosper, and as you wait on the Lord, be of good courage. God shall strengthen your heart! (Psalm 27)

JONCO PRODUCTIONS, INC./Sujay Ministries
1020 Grand Concourse – Suite S-2
Bronx, NY 10451
Telephone 718 537-7268   Fax 718 537-6945
www.drsujay.com

P R I C E   L I S T
BOOKS

Sister to Sister: Devotions for and from African American
Women (Judson) $11.00

Too Blessed to be Stressed: Words of Wisdom for Women
on the Move (Nelson) $14.00

Wise Women Bearing Gifts $11.00

Preaching in Two Voices: Sermons on The Women
In Jesus' Life (with William Watley) (Judson) $11.00

A New Dating Attitude: Getting Ready for the Mate God
Has for You (Zondervan) $14.00

Strengthened by the Struggle $11.00

Praying For The Men In Your Life (Zondervan) $10.99

The Sister's Rules For Ministry $10.00

VIDEO/AUDIO CASSETTES AND CDS

"Too Blessed to be Stressed," Woman, Thou Art Loosed
Conference - The Potter's House, July 2002
Video Cassette $20.00
Sermon: "Strengthened by the Struggle"
Audio . . . . $ 8.00
CD $10.00

OTHER MERCHANDISE
"Too Blessed to be Stressed" Mouse Pad . . $20.00
"Too Blessed to be Stressed" T-Shirt $15.00
"Strengthened by the Struggle" CD $10.00

Please make out cashier's check or money order to
JONCO PRODUCTIONS, INC.
Add $2 for shipping and handling

Thank you for your patronage.

JONCO